THE IMPORTANCE
OF BEING OSCAR

Micheál macLiammóir

R.H.A., I.A.L., LL.D. *Hon. Causa* T.C.D.

Winner :
The Douglas Hyde Award for Gaelic writing 1957
The Lady Gregory Medal of the Irish Academy of Letters 1960

Co-founder and director of the Dublin Gate Theatre

Chevalier de la Legion d'Honneur 1973
Freeman of the City of Dublin 1974

*

Born : Cork 1899
Died : Dublin 1978

MICHEÁL MacLIAMMÓIR

THE IMPORTANCE
OF BEING OSCAR

with an introduction by
HILTON EDWARDS

THE DOLMEN PRESS

Set in Baskerville type
and printed and published in the Republic of Ireland
at The Dolmen Press
North Richmond Industrial Estate, North Richmond St., Dublin 1

First edition: April 1963
Second edition revised and reset 1978

ISBN 0 85105 348 3

General distributors in North America:
Humanities Press Inc.
171 First Avenue, Atlantic Highlands, N.J. 07716

INTRODUCTION TO
The Importance of Being Oscar

❧

Under this title Micheál macLiammóir has selected and arranged, in a chronological pattern, excerpts from the poetry, prose, letters and dramatic writings of Oscar Wilde.

By the addition of a commentary, which conceals his scholarship under a mask of comedy, he has woven a tapestry which, as he unfolds it upon the stage, reaffirms Wilde as a master of English letters and the greatest wit of his generation, and vindicates the poet's dictum that he put his genius into his life.

As the pattern emerges it reveals both the brilliance and the self-destruction of that genius; an arabesque on the plane of the highest comedy which yet hints at the underlying seriousness of Wilde's curious and dangerous philosophy. It shows him to have been aware from the first of the inevitability of his tragedy, a fate which he appears deliberately to have sought with all the perversity of his extravagant nature, and leaves no doubt that, at his most triumphant moments he sensed the approach of the shadow that would at last envelop him.

There is no longer novelty in a solo performance. What gives *The Importance of Being Oscar* a unique quality is that macLiammóir's contribution, both as a writer and as an actor, not only confirms Wilde's stature as an artist, but relates his artistry to the now historic facts of his life; achieving what a distinguished dramatic critic has best described as: 'a new form: oral biography'.

It is as a biographer and a wit in his own right, as well as an actor, that macLiammóir holds the stage in this one-man *tour-de-force* which occupies, with a brief interval, something over two hours.

The success of *The Importance of Being Oscar* has been everywhere unquestioned. It was first presented in Dublin at the Gaiety Theatre as the Dublin Gate Theatre offering for the 1960 Theatre Festival, then transferred to London under the ægis of Sir Michael Redgrave and Mr. Fred Sadoff; first to the Apollo Theatre and later to the Royal Court Theatre. Both audience and press received it with enthusiasm.

An English tour was followed by a season at the Lyceum Theatre, New York, where the critical reception surpassed even London in its praise. After a tour of the United States there was an extended visit to the capitals of Latin America. At the Vieux Colombier in Paris, records were broken for that theatre. Then to Switzerland, Belgium and Holland, followed by Rome and Athens. Then a tour of South Africa followed by a still longer one to Australia and New Zealand, and short visits to Stockholm and Helsinki among other places, and various tours of England and the United States have confirmed a verdict of universal popularity and it seems that the demand for its continuance is not yet exhausted.

The performance has been televised by the Granada Network and recorded by the Columbia Company of America.

Now *The Importance of Being Oscar* appears in print, unassisted by the voice or the presence of its interpreter.

In this form it must necessarily have an effect altogether different from that of the theatrical performance for which it was intended, and it has been thought that some indication of how it was devised, of the personality of its originator and of the manner of its presentation on the stage, may be of service to the reader.

Actor, designer of settings and costumes, linguist and writer of plays and books both in Irish and in English, Micheál macLiammóir has given to the Dublin Gate Theatre, which he and I founded together in 1928, many

[6]

of those qualities for which it has gained some renown, and Trinity College, Dublin, has acknowledged his contribution to Irish life by conferring on him the Honorary degree of Doctor in Laws. macLiammóir's range as an actor equals the variety of his talents, but he possesses a gift for which the formality of the legitimate theatre seems to afford little scope. As much as an actor he is an entertainer; a raconteur. His clouded-velvet voice, his exceptional capacity for appreciation, his gaiety and ready wit, all tend to make him a spell-binder. Whatever his skill as an interpreter of the creations of others, he seems to attain fulfilment only when juggling with ideas and words of his own selection. The *Seanchai*, the storyteller, is a fast vanishing figure in the tradition of Gaelic and Irish culture. Oscar Wilde, though possibly unaware of it, owed much of his influence both as an artist and as a social lion to the craft of the *Seanchai*.

macLiammóir also shares something of the secret of this craft. Possessing a talent so little dependent upon the complex machinery of theatrical production, it is not surprising that he was urged to the consideration of a solo performance; to seek a form that would permit him a freedom larger than that of interpretation alone.

To begin with he toyed with the idea of what might be called an anthology of Irishry: an evening of Sheridan, Goldsmith, Merriman, Shaw, Wilde, Yeats, Synge and O'Casey. He hoped to include also Denis Johnston, Joyce and other modern Irish writers, but at that time neither he nor I had discovered a way of giving form and purpose to such a varied programme.*

It was when he was playing Judge Brack in *Hedda Gabler* with Peggy Ashcroft that he found in his pro-

*We now believe we have found a solution and since the success of *The Importance of Being Oscar*, macLiammóir has written and performed two other one-man shows: *I Must Be Talking to My Friends* (1963), an anthology of Irish writers in which the subject

[7]

ducer, Peter Ashmore, an equally ardent student of Wilde and I believe it was Peter Ashmore's suggestion that mac Liammóir devote his new performance to the Wilde Saga.

macLiammóir's interest in Wilde, his ill-starred fellow countryman, was of long standing. (At his instigation a sculptured stone plaque commemorating the centenary of Wilde's birth was placed upon the Dublin house in which he had been born.) So perhaps this was what we had been seeking; a focus upon one personality, and that an Irish writer of whom the actor had already made an extensive study.

Then came a doubt. Would an entire evening devoted to a single controversial figure of so heady a vintage be at once too limited and too cloying? Now such a doubt seems absurd: the problem soon became how to dis-embarrass ourselves of Wilde's riches.

We had always realised that Wilde, however wilfully he presented a premise, was seldom far from truth: that indeed his most apparently inconsequent utterance held almost invariably some deeper significance. Moreover,

---

was — instead of a person — Ireland herself; and a third, about William Butler Yeats.

Apart from tremendously diverting him and moving him to compassion, Wilde — macLiammóir always maintained — had no effect upon his life. What did influence him enormously and proved to be the lodestone that drew the young Irishman back to Ireland to devote himself to his native land was the writing of the poet, William Butler Yeats and, in his third one-man show, *Talking About Yeats* (1965), this is made manifest.

These two later shows, while not receiving the same wide acclaim as *The Importance of Being Oscar*, have proved very successful and were added to his repertoire, which he continued to play throughout the world, including several of the principal theatres in the West End of London and, indeed, his last performances in London were in the Haymarket and then the Duke of York's Theatre, with *Talking About Yeats*. The Duke of York's, incidentally, was the theatre in which he first played as a child in *Peter Pan*, thus bring-ing the wheel full circle.

that everything he wrote reflected, however mistily, an aspect of his life which, in turn, was always somewhere mirrored in his writing. As above, so below. Any concept of Wilde the artist was incomplete without reference to Wilde the man; any picture of Wilde himself inadequate without comprehension of his work. With so fabulous, so gay and yet so infinitely tragic a subject, what remained for macLiammóir but to apply to these elements his particular philosopher's stone?

In this way *The Importance of Being Oscar* developed, not just as a recital of prose and verse, nor as a mere lecture upon the consequences of a reckless life, but as a full-length portrait in pre-Raphaelite detail, such as Wilde himself tells us was painted of Dorian Gray; a portrait that, while it showed the sitter as he appeared to the world, gave evidence of his most secret act and thought.

As the project took shape I became convinced that in performance the actor's involvement must be limited: at no moment should the actor *play*, that is to say imper-sonate, Oscar Wilde. He could identify himself with Wilde's theories and emotions; he could temporarily become the characters of Wilde's creation, but he must never attempt to *be* Wilde but must remain always him-self. Stepping, as it were, in and out of the picture as occasion demanded he yet must always maintain an attitude aloof and ultimately objective; that of the Teller of the Story, of the *Seanchaí*. Only then, I felt certain, would he be able to establish intimacy with his audience; to forge a link between them and his subject and still be free to comment.

Further, if the performance was not to lack visual interest it must be given a shape that it could retain even after constant repetition. Something more was necessary than for the actor, just because he was alone, merely to stand or sit upon the stage or to wander as the spirit moved him.

[9]

A plan of movement must be designed that would have purpose and significance, that would defeat monotony and be both pleasing and effective. This presented problems because of the limited pattern that can be made by a single figure alone upon a stage.

Above all, everything must appear to be spontaneous, as if unrehearsed, and this effect could only be maintained consistently as the result of a planned artifice which is the reverse of chance.

Finally, what was the entertainment to look like? Where should it appear to take place? Upon an empty, curtained stage or in a set representing, for instance, a room? The first would be deadly dull, the latter too confining. So we devised a shadowy space representing no locality, furnished with the bare essentials to performance but avoiding austerity. Austerity and Wilde would surely be strange bed-fellows.

A table, a sofa, a chair and a floor covering designed to bind them together. Then (the one concession to ornament, which was also to strike the keynote to each half of the show), a pedestal on which was an urn of great waxen, moonlit lilies, a symbol at once decorative and macabre. These, for the second part of the performance, as the shadow of Nemesis crept closer, were to be replaced by autumn leaves: 'yellow and black and pale and hectic red'.

A moonlit space surrounding the gold of lamplight; a setting utterly simple and at the same time sybaritic but which commits the action to no definite locality.

The American dramatic critic, Howard Taubman, gives this impression of the first appearance on Broadway of *The Importance of Being Oscar* in a review in the *New York Times* of 15th March 1961:

'It is a virtuoso performance. . . . But even as he performs, Mr. macLiammóir preserves a strong measure of his own identity. Unlike other one-man shows devoted to recalling the person and creative world of a renowned writer, Mr. macLiammóir's does not attempt to assume his subject's appearance. . . . He is elucidator as well as protagonist, generous critic as well as versatile actor.

'The visual aids Mr. macLiammóir summons to his side are modest indeed. A black cloth frames the stage. The simple but elegant furnishings . . . give the stage the appearance of an ambience of a special time and yet free of time. Mr. macLiammóir himself is in a dinner jacket and black tie. What he communicates is the sum of his gift as an artist and an ardent interpreter of Wilde.

'The shadows close in as the first half ends . . . when he returns the lilies in the vase have been replaced by trailing autumn leaves. Mr. macLiammóir himself stands in a sombre half light, his head bowed, like a man who has been through purgatory.

'Although the mood of the second part is grave, Mr. macLiammóir takes care to light it with flashes of Wilde's humour. . . . He does not spare Wilde nor does he judge him. He reveals him affectionately. He is an Irishman proudly proclaiming a compatriot's expression, in himself and in his work, of the spirit of Ireland. . . . Mr. macLiammóir has created a vivid and memorable evening in the theatre.'

We are grateful to Oscar Wilde's son, Mr. Vyvyan Holland, for permitting us the use, in performance and in publication here, of those extracts from his father's letters which have provided such an essential and poignant contribution to this anthology; particularly those portions of De Profundis so long kept secret. We believe that the magic of Oscar Wilde together with the sincerity of this tribute to him will assure that the absence of a performer, a director and a theatre will be no impediment to the reader's appreciation of *The Importance of Being Oscar*. macLiammóir last performed *The Importance of Being Oscar* at his own Gate Theatre in Dublin for a week in December 1975 on the eve of his entering hospital for a serious operation.

His performance was perhaps slower and less sparkling than previously, but had achieved a depth and intensity that was magical, and each night he received a standing ovation.

It was almost as if the audience realised the significance of the occasion: a triumphant conclusion to a brilliant career. He ended as if with an accolade.

HILTON EDWARDS

Micheál macLiammóir

IN HIS

The Importance of
Being Oscar

(The Wit, Triumph and Tragedy of Oscar Wilde)

DIRECTED BY HILTON EDWARDS

❧

The Importance of Being Oscar *was performed by the author, devised and directed by Hilton Edwards, decorated by Molly MacEwen, and first presented by The Dublin Theatre Festival at The Gaiety Theatre, Dublin, on 19 September 1960.*

It has been played in several London theatres, in New York, Paris, and on tour in Britain, South America, the United States of America, Europe, South Africa, Australia and New Zealand.

Micheál macLiammóir gave his final performances of The Importance of Being Oscar *at the Gate Theatre, Dublin, during December 1975.*

The production was televised by RTE in Dublin, and recorded by CBS records.

❧

PART ONE

The Happy Prince & The Green Carnation

Hélas · Introduction to an Aesthete · Lily Langtry · Art in Leadville · The Green Carnation · Lord Goring and a Buttonhole · The Harlot's House · The Picture of Dorian Gray · Lord Alfred · Art and Life · The Jewels of Herod · A Telegram to the Sphinx · Lady Bracknell Says 'No' · The Last First Night · A Bouquet from the Marquis · A Letter to Robert Ross.

The trials of Oscar Wilde
may be supposed to take place
during the interval

PART TWO

De Profundis

The Sentence · Conjecture · Ross receives Instructions · De Profundis · Literature and the Warder · A Welcome from the Sphinx · With André Gide at Berneval · Return to Lord Alfred · The Ballad of Reading Gaol · Aftermath · The rue des Beaux Arts · Prose Poem on the Boulevard des Italiens · The Curtain falls in the Hôtel d'Alsace.

PART ONE

The Happy Prince & The Green Carnation

❧

HÉLAS!

To drift with every passion till my soul
Is a stringed lute on which all winds can play.
Is it for this that I have given away
Mine ancient wisdom, and austere control?
Methinks my life is a twice-written scroll
Scrawled over on some boyish holiday
With idle songs for pipe and virelay.
Which do but mar the secret of the whole.
Surely there was a time I might have trod
The sunlit heights, and from Life's dissonance
Struck one clear chord to reach the ears of God:
Is that time dead? lo! with a little rod
I did but touch the honey of romance —
And must I lose a soul's inheritance?

❧

For a long time before that poem had appeared in print
its author's name was providing the English public with
a topic for conversation very far removed indeed from
its normal subjects, at once so classic and so cosy, of the
Weather and the Royal Family.

'There goes that bloody fool Oscar Wilde,' a gentleman
in the street had audibly remarked as he passed the poet
by, and the poet turned to his companion and said: 'It is
quite extraordinary how quickly one becomes known in
London.'

His appearance, of course, in these early days in

[15]

London, was spectacular . . . we can picture the tall, amply-built young man, with that powerful, indolent, putty-coloured, Babylonian sort of a face he had with its drooping crown of long dim hair into which, at some moment of depression perhaps, the iron had entered: often he would be wearing knee breeches, silk stockings, a velvet coat, a floating tie of greenish brocaded satin, and in one pale, pointed hand there would be a lily, sometimes even a sunflower. . . . Well, he was bound to attract attention. And this made him exquisitely happy: to pass unnoticed anywhere would have seemed to him a most ostentatious form of obscurity. As he said himself in later years: 'I have no wish to pose as being ordinary, great Heaven!'

Indeed the one ordinary thing Oscar Wilde seems to have done in his life was to have fled away from his native Ireland as soon as he possibly could. This, of course, was pretty ordinary in every sense of the word, because for one thing, you see, everybody was doing it. Oh yes, I assure you, in those days every young Irish man, particularly if he had any literary or imaginative talent or ambition, seems to have left the unfortunate country as soon as he had had his first shave, and for once Oscar Wilde was no exception to the Irish rule. He wanted something, of course, that he realised his own native city, the impoverished capital of an impoverished nation, could never have given him. He wanted world-wide fame, and he decided to begin by being talked about everywhere in the world.

Now Dublin, doubtless, would have talked about him too. Dublin, indeed, had done so already, he had seen to that: but in Dublin talk was merely for talk's sake: there would have been no result of the talk at all: no world-wide fame, no rich reward, no jewelled elegance, and the dinner tables he so rightly felt himself destined to dominate would have been in Dublin at once less opulent than those in London and far more conversationally competitive. . . . A very charming and rather busy English lady, once gently rebuking the poet for his faith in a fortune teller, had said: 'Fortune telling? Oh but deep down do you not think that is rather tempting Providence, Mr. Wilde?' And he had answered: 'Dear lady, surely Providence can resist temptation by this time.'

Now who in his own Ireland would have listened to a crack like that without either trying to cap or capsize it? Ah no; wealthy, good-natured, tongue-tied England was clearly the place for him, and to England he went, and having emerged from Oxford encrusted with honours, he settled down in London where he found time to amuse himself — and the town — prodigiously; to lecture about art, to be invited to dine at nearly every great house in Mayfair—quite often more than once—and also to write a quantity of verse.

In London he found time, too, to fall in love with the beautiful Mrs. Langtry, the glorious, the notorious Lily Langtry, the Jersey Lily as she was sometimes called, and he even found time to pass a night or two — once we are told he chose a snowy night — passionately asleep on her doorstep (outside the house of course!). On the snowy occasion the lone and palely slumbering poet was stumbled over by Mr. Langtry who was returning from his club late and possibly rather merry. She, *la Belle Dame sans Merci*, allowed the poet to worship her through one mad marvellous summer, and then she advised him not to waste his time. I don't think he was wasting time at all for he left some charming poems in celebration of her astonishing beauty and to one of these poems he gave no title at all. He dedicated it simply 'To L.L.', the initials, of course, of his beloved.

. . . I remember we used to meet
By an ivied seat.
And you warbled each pretty word
With the air of a bird:

And your voice had a quaver in it,
Just like a linnet,
And shook, as the blackbird's throat
With its last big note:

And your eyes, they were green and grey
Like an April day,
But lit into amethyst
When I stooped and kissed:

And your mouth, it would never smile
For a long, long while,
Then it rippled all over with laughter
Five minutes after.

You were always afraid of a shower,
Just like a flower:
I remember you started and ran
When the rain began.

*   *   *

I remember so well the room,
And the lilac bloom
That beat at the dripping pane
In the warm June rain:

And the colour of your gown,
It was amber-brown,
And two yellow satin bows
From your shoulders rose.

And the handkerchief of French lace
Which you held to your face . . .
Had a small tear left a stain?
Or was it the rain?

On your hand as it waved adieu
There were veins of blue,
In your voice as it said good-bye
Was a petulant cry.

'You have only wasted your life.'
(Ah, that was the knife!)
When I rushed through the garden gate
It was all too late.

*   *   *

Well, if my heart must break,
Dear love, for your sake,
It will break in music, I know
Poet's hearts break so.

But strange that I was not told
That the brain can hold
In a tiny ivory cell
God's heaven and hell.

Was it prophetic that last verse? One wonders. Yet how joyful even an unrequited passion made the poet in those youthful days, when he himself was indeed the Happy Prince of his own fable, and as if to prove his curious theory that it is only 'shallow love that lives forever', he recovered with remarkable rapidity from the heart that Lily Langtry had broken, and he journeyed most cheerfully to America to lecture on Art and Aesthetics.

[19]

He was now twenty-eight years old, and having expressed a faint disapproval of the Atlantic Ocean. . . . 'I am disappointed with the Atlantic,' he confessed. 'It is not as majestic, or even as large, as I had expected': and having told some New York Customs official on arrival that he had 'nothing to declare but his genius', having said these things, he proceeded to give to his trans-Atlantic audience all they expected and perhaps a little more. Here are some of his own impressions of the remoter parts of Colorado in the early 1880's:

'While I was lecturing at Denver,' he writes, 'I received a message that if I went on to Leadville, as I proposed to do, the harsher spirits in that wild mining town would be sure to shoot me or my travelling manager. I wrote and told them that nothing they could possibly do to my travelling manager would intimidate me. And I went. It was a gloomy jolting journey on a gloomy wet day, 150 miles through the Rocky Mountains, and one arrived at last at a cheerless snow-covered station. At my lecture the following night a baby was present, and when I said: "There is no better way of loving nature than through Art" the baby burst into tears. I said: "I wish the juvenile enthusiast would restrain its aesthetic raptures" and all was silent. My audience otherwise was mainly composed of silver miners whose huge sombre hats, scarlet shirts and high boots made me think of seventeenth century Cavaliers. Indeed they were the first really well-dressed men I had seen since my arrival in the United States. They sat there, rows and rows of them, enormous, powerfully-built men, silent as the grave, their eyes watchful, their brawny arms folded over their muscular chests, a loaded gun on each swelling thigh.

'I spoke to these delightful fellows about the early Florentine schools of painting, and they slept as peacefully as though no crime had ever stained the ravines of their mountain home. I described to them the pictures of Botticelli and the name, that seemed to them like a newly-invented drink, roused them from their dreams. I read them passages from the autobiography of that great Florentine genius and adventurer Benvenuto Cellini, and he proved so popular that they asked as one man "Why the hell I had not brought him with me?" I explained that Benvenuto had been dead for some years, which elicited the immediate demand: "Who shot him?"

'They then invited me to supper, and having accepted I had to descend a mine in a rickety bucket in which it was utterly impossible . . . even for me . . . to be graceful. At the bottom of the mine we sat down to the banquet, the first course being whiskey, the second whiskey, and the third whiskey. The amazement of the miners when they saw that Art and appetite could go hand in hand knew no bounds: when I lit a long cigar and quaffed a couple of cocktails without flinching they cheered me till the silver fell in glittering dust from the roof on to our table. . . .'

Incidentally, Oscar Wilde, it is said, drank those rough fellows under that very table on that very night, and many other people under many other tables on many other rough nights. He seems indeed to have had a perfectly splendid time all over the United States, and it is delightful to reflect that among the many distinguished Americans who welcomed him to their country were Walt Whitman, Mark Twain, and who do you think? Now who? The authoress of *Little Women* and *Good Wives*. What Miss Louisa May Alcott thought of Mr. Oscar Wilde, or indeed what Oscar thought of Louisa May, history, alas, has never related.

When he got back to London he fell in love all over again. And this time he married her: a gentle and very beautiful Irish girl called Constance Mary Lloyd. They were passionately and mutually in love and supremely happy, and at the same time Wilde was making his first experiments in the art of the dramatist. His first two plays were what today would be, I fear, briefly and brutally described as Flops; but soon he produced a resounding success called *Lady Windermere's Fan*. And this comedy of manners it was that first set the seal of a wide popularity upon an already considerable reputation in the world of literature and art and that earned for him too the cachet of an elegant modernity. He was regarded indeed by his contemporaries as representing the quintessence of an almost dangerous ultra-modernism, and to my mind the essential modern who happens also to be a man of genius is not content with merely echoing the age he lives in: he invents it. Aesthetically speaking Oscar Wilde, I seriously suggest to you, was largely responsible for the invention of the period we speak of today as the 1890's, through the first half of which remarkable decade he strutted, and through the second half of which . . . he staggered.

The strutting phase, when he was dandy of dress, dandy of speech, dandy of manner, dandy of wit, dandy even of ideas and intellect . . . the period, in fact, during which he invented that curious dyed flower, forever associated with his name — the Green Carnation — has a characteristic moment in a little scene from his comedy *An Ideal Husband*, a scene which opens with Lord Goring, between two London parties, explaining to his manservant, Phipps, the subtle influence of the Buttonhole on Thought. Lord Goring enters in a white tie with a rather faded flower in his coat that he wants to change for the second party and, seeing his man standing there, he says to him:

LORD GORING   Got my second buttonhole for me, Phipps?
PHIPPS   Yes, my lord.
LORD GORING   Rather distinguished thing, Phipps. I am the only person of the smallest importance in London at present who wears a buttonhole.

PHIPPS   Yes, my lord. I have observed that.

GORING   You see, Phipps, Fashion is what one wears oneself. What is unfashionable is what other people wear.

PHIPPS   Yes, my lord.

GORING   Just as vulgarity is simply the conduct of other people.

PHIPPS   Yes, my lord.

GORING   And falsehood the truth of other people.

PHIPPS   Yes, my lord.

GORING   Other people are quite dreadful, Phipps. The only possible society is oneself.

PHIPPS   Yes, my lord.

GORING   To love oneself is the beginning of a lifelong romance, Phipps.

PHIPPS   Yes, my lord.

GORING   (*looking at himself in the glass*)   Don't think I quite like this buttonhole, Phipps. Makes me look a little too old. Makes me almost in the prime of life, eh, Phipps? For the future a more trivial buttonhole, perhaps, on Thursday evenings.

PHIPPS   I will speak to the florist, my lord. She has had a loss in her family lately, which perhaps accounts for the lack of triviality your lordship complains of in the buttonhole.

GORING   Extraordinary thing about the lower classes in England — they are always losing their relations.

PHIPPS   Yes, my lord. They are extremely fortunate in that respect.

GORING   H'm . . . ! Want my cab round at once. If anyone else calls I am not at home. Thank you, Phipps, that will do. . . . Phipps' views on family life seem somewhat lax. Really, if one's own servants don't set one a good moral example, what on earth is the use of them?

PHIPPS   Ahem! Lord Caversham!

GORING Ah! Why will one's parents always appear at the wrong time? Some extraordinary mistake in nature, I suppose . . . Delighted to see you, my dear father.

CAVERSHAM Take my cloak off.

GORING Is it really worth while, father?

CAVERSHAM Of course it is worth while, sir. Which is the most comfortable chair in the room?

GORING This one, father. It is the chair I use myself when I have visitors.

CAVERSHAM Thank ye. No draughts, I hope, in this room?

GORING No, father.

CAVERSHAM Glad to hear it. . . . Want to have a serious conversation with you, sir.

GORING My dear father! A serious conversation? At this hour? Why it is long after seven and my doctor says I must not have any serious conversation after seven. It makes me talk in my sleep.

CAVERSHAM Talk in your sleep, sir? What does that matter? You are not married.

GORING No, father, I am not married.

CAVERSHAM Hum! That is what I have come to talk to you about, sir. You have got to get married and at once. Why dammit, sir, look at me! Why, when I was your age, sir, I had been an inconsolable widower for three months, and was already paying my addresses to your admirable mother. Damme, sir, it is your duty to get married. You can't be always living for pleasure. High time you got a wife, sir. You are thirty-four years of age.

GORING Yes, father, but I only admit to thirty-two — thirty-one and a half when there are pink shades on the lights and I have a really good buttonhole. This buttonhole is not . . . trivial enough.

CAVERSHAM I tell you you are thirty-four, sir. (*Sneeze*) And, what is more, there *is* a draught in your room.

Why did you tell me there was no draught, sir? I feel it. I feel it distinctly.

GORING So do I, father. It is a dreadful draught. Dear father, do let me take you to the smoking-room. Your sneezes are quite heart-rending.

CAVERSHAM Well, sir, I suppose I have a right to sneeze when I choose?

GORING Quite so, father. I was merely expressing sympathy.

CAVERSHAM Oh, damn sympathy! There is a great deal too much of that sort of thing going on in London nowadays. . . .

GORING I quite agree with you, father. If there was less sympathy in the world there would be less trouble in the world.

CAVERSHAM Tell me, do you always understand what you are talking about, sir?

GORING (*after some hesitation*) Yes, father, if I listen attentively.

CAVERSHAM If you listen attentively! . . . Conceited young puppy!

With his growing success as a playwright, a curious new note could be seen gradually developing in the personality of Oscar Wilde. One might say — rather fancifully, if you will — that the joyous, pagan noonday of his Sunflower and Lily were making way for the more subtle, elaborate afternoon of his Green Carnation. The Green Carnation by this time in fact had come to mean something much more than a mere buttonhole, and stood for a brief and brilliant season or two as the symbol of the age. And it seems to me that it represented a mood rather than a movement: a mood that was at once indolent, voluptuous, bizarre, witty and deliberately artificial. To many people it seemed a delightful affair, this hilarious revolt against Victorianism, others found in the Green Carnation something faintly sinister.

But nobody denied that the Green Carnation represented a significant though fleeting moment in the history of intellectual fashions, and nobody denied that Wilde was the high priest of that moment. One of his poems — written, indeed, before he had invented what he called 'That magnificent flower'—nevertheless reveals one aspect of its many moods in a capricious and macabre light. . . .

> We caught the tread of dancing feet.
> We loitered down the moonlit street,
> And stopped beneath the harlot's house.
>
> Inside, above the din and fray,
> We heard the loud musicians play
> The 'Treues liebes Herz' of Strauss.
>
> Like strange mechanical grotesques,
> Making fantastic arabesques,
> The shadows raced across the blind.
>
> We watched the ghostly dancers spin
> To sound of horn and violin,
> Like black leaves wheeling in the wind.
>
> *   *   *
>
> Sometimes a clockwork puppet pressed
> A phantom lover to her breast,
> Sometimes they seemed to try to sing.
>
> Sometimes a horrible marionette
> Came out, and smoked its cigarette
> Upon the steps like a live thing.

Then, turning to my love, I said,
'The dead are dancing with the dead,
The dust is whirling with the dust.'

But she — she heard the violin,
And left my side, and entered in:
Love passed into the house of lust.

Then suddenly the tune went false,
The dancers wearied of the waltz,
The shadows ceased to wheel and whirl.

And down the long and silent street,
The dawn, with silver-sandalled feet,
Crept like a frightened girl.

The same curious mood had found a fuller expression in his one and only novel, a work which earned for him the almost unanimous abuse of all the critics. It was considered by them and by a vast number of the public that the book was unwholesome. 'Unwholesome', of course, was a favourite adjective of the period. Anything you disapproved of you said was 'Unwholesome sir: Unwholesome!' and you snorted. If, however, you were the sort of person who did approve of that sort of thing, you said it was 'deliciously, deciduously exotic' and you tossed your head, gazed at the ceiling, and breathed through your nose. So you see people haven't changed a bit really. Anyway, this particular work of art was indeed delicious, deciduous, unwholesome, exotic, anything you like, and the thing played Old Harry for many a long day with late Victorian susceptibilities. Although the odd thing, as Wilde himself pointed out in its defence, is that in actual fact the story contains a quite obvious and rather terrible moral. As you will see.

The famous painter, Basil Hallward, at work in his London studio, is putting the last touches to a splendid full-length portrait in modern dress of a young gentleman who is twenty years old, who is the possessor of birth, breeding, of immense wealth, of astonishing physical beauty, and who bears the name of Dorian Gray. The painter, Hallward, feels a certain romantic admiration for his sitter, and, entirely against his own better judgement, he introduces the boy one exquisite day in summer to an old Oxford friend of his own called Lord Henry Wotton. Now Lord Henry Wotton is simply Mephistopheles in *Faust*: that who he is, plain as a pikestaff, and the moment he sets eyes on Dorian Gray he proceeds to pour into the lad's youthful ears his own peculiar philosophy of living. This, briefly, is that youth and pleasure and beauty, however fleeting, are the only things in the world worth a damn, and that the best way to enjoy them to the full is by draining every cup life can offer to the dregs. Dorian, timidly but with no hesitation at all, becomes a convert to this Hedonistic viewpoint, and when Hallward's portrait of him is finished and he, standing in front of it, realises completely for the first time how amazingly young and how ridiculously handsome he is — like some Greek god — he utters a prayer. And he prays that the picture may change with the passing of the years, that the picture may grow old and ugly and bear the visible burden of all his days and all his deeds and that he himself, no matter what he may choose to do with his life, may remain forever young and beautiful.

'When the Gods wish to punish us they answer our prayers', Wilde had said. And that is what happens to the hero of the novel. His prayer is answered, the miracle happens: the picture does begin to change, subtly, rather horribly, and Dorian, frightened by the alteration that is creeping over the painted canvas, has the uncanny thing hidden away in an attic at the top of his great house in Grosvenor Square in London, an attic to which he alone holds the key. And then, largely under the influence of an evil but fascinating book — French, of course — given to him by Lord Henry Wotton — of course — largely under this baleful influence Dorian Gray begins to lead a life of the most reprehensible, though on the whole unspecified pleasures, passing from pleasure to dubious pleasure, and from one strange forbidden erotic vice to another. And yet, in spite of the passing of many years, and of the really dreadful life he is leading, Dorian Gray goes on looking like a blameless young Narcissus.

The same, alas, cannot be said of the portrait, which all alone in its locked-up attic, (with an occasional visit from Dorian to see how it is getting along) the portrait, as the years roll by, goes from beautiful to bad and from bad to worse. The painted body grows fat with luxury, the painted face cadaverous with sin, the eyes burn in their sockets; the slowly increasing depravity of the thing is horrifying. Oh well . . . nineteen Baroque years go by in this fashion, and the innocent cause of all the trouble, Basil Hallward, who painted the fatal picture, is perturbed by the evil reputation that by this time inevitably has fastened itself upon the name of Dorian Gray. So perturbed indeed is good staunch friend Basil Hallward that one foggy November night he calls on Dorian at Grosvenor Square and asks him point blank is there any truth at all in the hideous rumours that are circulating about him everywhere.

Dorian is furious with Hallward: he is incensed by what he considers a vulgar and impertinent cross-examination, and suddenly he says: 'Very well, Basil! As you seem so concerned about my life, I think you might as well know everything. Come with me. Come upstairs. I keep a diary of my life from day to day and it never leaves the room in which it is written. Come with me. You have chattered long enough tonight about corruption. Well, now you shall look on corruption, face to face.'

And he takes up a lamp and guides the bewildered Hallward up the stairs. As he unlocks the door of the attic he looks again at his friend and says: 'As a matter of fact, Basil, you of all men have a right to know everything about me. Everything. You have had much more to do with my life than you have ever dreamend.'

The two men enter the attic together and Hallward sees to his astonishment that he is in a barely furnished room, dim with dust and cobwebs, and that there, facing him on the wall, is a full-length portrait of a grey, stooping, elderly man, with the face, the eyes and the mouth of an evil satyr. Slowly he understands. It is the picture of Dorian Gray which he himself painted nearly twenty years ago. Overwhelmed by loathing and revulsion he turns, more furious than before, on the golden-haired young Apollo who stands at his side and says: 'Dorian! . . . But if this is true — if it can be true — and this is what you are doing to your life — to your soul — Dorian!'

The quarrel blazes up between the two and after a few moments in an excess of loathing of this man who he feels has ruined his life and is now lecturing him about it, Dorian rushes suddenly upon Hallward, who sat at the table, his face buried in his hands, and dug the knife into the great vein that is behind the ear, crushing the man's head down on the table, and stabbing him again and again.

There was the horrible sound of someone choking with blood. Three times the outstretched arms shot up convulsively. He stabbed him twice more, but now the man did not move. He was dead. . . . And yet had it not been for the red jagged tear in the neck, and the clotted black pool that was slowly brimming over the table edge, one would have said that he was simply asleep. . . .

How quickly it had all been done! Dorian Gray felt

strangely calm, and, walking over to the window, he opened it, and stepped out on to the balcony. The air!

The wind had blown the fog away, and the sky was like a monstrous peacock's tail, starred with myriads of golden eyes.

He looked down, and saw a policeman going his rounds, flashing the long beam of his lantern on the doors of the silent houses. The crimson spot of a prowling hansom gleamed at the corner and then vanished. A woman in a fluttering shawl was creeping slowly by the railings, staggering as she went. Now and then she stopped, and peered back into the darkness. Once she began to sing in a hoarse voice. The policeman strolled over and said something to her. She stumbled away, laughing. . . . A bitter blast swept across the square. The gas-lamps flickered and became blue, and the leafless trees shook their black, iron branches to and fro. He shivered and went back, closing the window behind him.

The dead thing was still seated in the chair, half sprawling over the table with long fantastic arms and bowed head glistening with blood. Basil Hallward . . . he was nothing now but a dreadful white wax image.

His eyes fell on the picture. What was that crimson dew that spotted the right hand? Blood, oozing from the painted canvas. . . .

He turned away and leaned his forehead against the cold mist-stained glass of the window-panes. Then, for some reason, he pulled out his watch. It was twenty minutes to two. And Dorian Gray began to think — to think — to think. . . .

Dorian Gray, with the aid of a scientific friend, whom he blackmails that he may help him in this work, disposes by fire of the body of Basil Hallward, the artist and the devoted friend he has murdered. And then in complete safety he continues for a while to lead his elaborately evil life. But only for a while. Slowly, inevitably, it palls on

[31]

him. Slowly, inevitably, the image of corruption and decay at work in his soul rises like a phantom and looks him in the eyes. Then, suddenly one day, his tortured imagination is purified by a new thought — a very simple thought — a form of resolution, a childlike dream for the future. And filled with the freshness and the beauty that this new hope seems to offer him in life, he finds himself one lovely night in summer about six months after the murder of Basil Hallward, dining alone with his old friend, Lord Henry Wotton, at Lord Henry's house in Curzon Street. And as dinner draws towards its close he confides to his host his new decision about the manner of his future life.

'There is no use your telling me that you are going to be good, my dear Dorian,' cried Lord Henry, dipping his fingers into a red copper bowl filled with rose-water. 'You're quite perfect. Pray, don't change.'

'No, Harry, I have done too many evil things in my life. Evil. You don't know the twentieth part of that side of my life, Harry. I think that if you did, even you would turn away from me. You laugh. You mustn't laugh. Well, I've changed. . . . I'm going to lead a completely new life. Oh I know I've told you that already. But there's something I haven't told you. I've begun already . . . oh for some time now and I've . . . oh Harry! Harry! . . . if you're going to laugh about it let's talk of something else. Please! Tell me something about yourself. What is going on in town? I have not been to the club for ages.'

'The Club? Oh! People are still discussing poor Basil's disappearance.'

'Basil Hallward? Really? I should have thought they had got tired of that subject by this time.'

'My dear Dorian, they have only been talking about it for six weeks, and the British public are really not equal to the mental strain of having more than one topic every six months. They have had my own divorce case, and now they have got the mysterious disappearance of a famous artist. You see, Dorian, Scotland Yard still insists that the tall man in the grey ulster who left for Paris by the midnight train on the ninth of November was Basil, and the French police declare that Basil never arrived in Paris at all. I suppose in about a fortnight we shall be told that he has been seen in San Francisco. Yes. . . . It's an odd thing, but everyone who disappears nowadays is said to be seen, sooner or later, in San Francisco. It must be a delightful city, and possess all the attractions of the next world. Let us have our coffee in the music room, Dorian. You must play Chopin to me. I adore Chopin. The man with whom my wife ran away played Chopin exquisitely!'

Dorian said nothing, but rose from the table and, passing into the next room, sat down to the piano. After the coffee had been brought in he stopped playing and looking over at Lord Henry, he said suddenly: 'Harry, did it ever occur to you that Basil was murdered?'

'Oh, Basil had no enemies. Though I will admit he was thoroughly disliked by all his friends. No: he was really rather popular wasn't he? And always wore a Waterbury watch. Dear Basil! Why should he have been murdered?'

'What would you say, Harry, if I told you that I had murdered Basil?'

'I would say, my dear fellow, that you were posing for a character that doesn't suit you. It is not in you, Dorian, to commit a murder. I am sorry if I hurt your vanity by saying so, but I assure you it is true. All crime is vulgar, just as all vulgarity is crime. Besides, crime is essentially the prerogative of the lower classes. I don't blame them for it in the least. I should imagine that crime was to them what art is to us: simply a method of seeking extraordinary sensations.'

'Sensations? You don't really think that a man who

[33]

once, in a moment of passion, had committed a murder could possibly do the same thing again? Don't tell me you believe that.'

'My dear boy, anything becomes a pleasure if one does it once too often. But murder, I should fancy, is invariably rather a mistake. One should never do anything that one cannot talk about after dinner. No, let us pass from poor Basil. I wish I could believe that he had come to such a really romantic end as you suggest: but I can't. I daresay he fell into the Seine off an omnibus, and that the conductor hushed up the scandal. The French are so tactful. . . . But if he is dead I don't want to think about him. Death terrifies me. I hate it. Death and vulgarity are the only two facts the nineteenth century has not yet explained away. Why are you so serious? Play me something. Play me a nocturne, Dorian, and as you play, tell me, in a low voice, how you have kept your youth. Don't look so terrified, my dear boy. Obviously you must have some secret. You really are very wonderful, Dorian. You look tonight as you always look: the same boy that I met in Basil's garden. And that was twenty years ago. It's incredible. I wish you would tell me your secret. To get back my youth I would do anything in the world, except get up early, take exercise, or be respectable. I have sorrows, Dorian, that even you know nothing of. The tragedy of old age is not that one is old, but that one is young. I am amazed sometimes at my own sincerity. Ah, Dorian, how happy you are! What an exquisite life you have had! You have known everything. You have drunk deeply of everything. And yet life has not changed you. You are still the same.'

'I am not the same, Harry. I've changed — and I'm going to change more than ever.'

'You cannot change to me, Dorian. You and I will always be friends.'

'Yes, I suppose we will. . . . And yet you poisoned me

[34]

with a book once. I should never forgive you for that. . . . Harry, promise me that you will never give that book to anyone else. Promise me. It does harm to people's souls.'

'My dear boy, you are actually beginning to moralise. Soon you will be going about warning people against all the sins of which you have grown tired. You are much too delightful to play the hypocrite. As for being poisoned by a book, there is no such thing as that. Art has no influence upon action. Art annihilates the desire to act. It is superby sterile. The books the world calls immoral are the books that show the world its own shame. That is all. Are you going already? But why? Then lunch with me tomorrow. . . . No, no, no, I'll call for you, of course, at a quarter past one. Goodnight, Dorian.'

'Goodnight, Harry.' But as Dorian Gray got up to the door he hesitated as though there were something he must say to his friend. Then he sighed, and went out.

It was an exquisite summer's night and as he strolled home he began to think again about his new resolution; to wonder, if he succeeded in making his life pure and whole again, would he ever be able to banish that look of nameless evil from the painted face in the locked-up room. He paused. Perhaps with the very birth of his resolution, with the new life he had been leading, yes . . . perhaps the signs of evil were already fading from the canvas. Perhaps the picture was beginning to change once more. He would go and look.

So when he arrived at his house he sent his servant to bed, and taking a lamp he crept softly upstairs. He passed swiftly into the attic, locking and bolting the door behind him, as was his custom, and placing the lamp on the table, he looked at the picture. No change. No change at all . . . save that in the eyes there was a new and horrifying expression of cunning, and on the mouth the curved wrinkle of the hypocrite. . . . So Lord Henry had been right. There was nothing in his new resolution but hypocrisy. The thing was still loathsome — more loathsome, if possible, than before — and the scarlet dew that spotted the hand seemed brighter than ever and more than ever like blood newly spilt. There was blood too on the painted feet, as though the thing had dripped . . . blood even on the hand that had not held the knife. . . .

What did it mean? That he was to confess to the murder of Basil Hallward? To give himself up, and be put to death? He laughed. The idea was grotesque. Why should he confess? There was no evidence against him. No evidence against Dorian Gray . . . except that. The picture itself—with its leering face and its blood-dripping hands — that was the only evidence in the world against him. He would destroy it.

He looked round, and saw the knife that had stabbed Basil Hallward. As it had killed the painter, so it would kill the painter's work and all that that meant. It would kill his conscience. Well, he would live without his conscience, he would live without his soul, and when their hideous warnings were silent he would be free. He seized the knife and stabbed the picture with it.

There was a great cry heard, so horrible in its agony that the frightened servants woke and crept in silence, one by one, from their rooms. Then they began talking in low whispers to each other. After a little, three of the men servants mounted the great staircase. They knocked at the door of the attic, but there was no reply. They called aloud, 'Mr. Dorian! Mr. Dorian!' The house was as silent as a tomb. Finally, after vainly trying to force the door, they climbed on the roof and dropped down on to the balcony. The windows yielded easily: their bolts were old.

When the men entered they found, hanging upon the wall, a splendid portrait of their master as they had last seen him on that very day in all the wonder of his golden youth and beauty. Lying on the floor was a dead man,

[36]

in evening dress, with a knife in his heart. He was old, withered, wrinkled, and loathsome of visage. It was not till the men had examined the rings on his fingers that they realised who it was.

❧

For the author of *The Decay of Lying*, an essay in which Wilde sets forth his famous theory that, far from Art's 'Holding the mirror up to Nature', it is in fact, he assured his startled generation, 'really Nature — and indeed Life — who, in their own clumsy, old-fashioned way, do their best to follow Art. . . . London fogs, for example,' he declared, 'were simply Nature's unfortunate amateurish attempt to imitate the French impressionists. . . .' Well, for the author of such an astonishing theory, I say, it must have been an astonishing experience to meet, for the first time in his life and well over a year after the publication of Dorian Gray, with Dorian Gray. 'His name, of course, was not Dorian Gray.' His name was Lord Alfred Douglas — known to his family and friends as Bosie — and he bore the most amazing resemblance to the hero of the novel. But unlike Dorian, who never did anything with his strange and sinister life except to be Dorian, Lord Alfred was a poet, and a considerable poet. Curiously enough, and as I think, sadly and significantly enough, Oscar Wilde, almost as soon as his famous and fatal friendship with this young man had begun, himself ceased almost entirely to write poetry. His whole attention was focussed now upon the stage and — as I think for the first time — on life, 'that tiger life' as he was to call it in later years; and for the moment life itself and the stage alike meant to Oscar Wilde the spirit of laughter, the spirit of comedy.

Only one work appeared during these years that was not dictated by the spirit of laughter and that work —

finished just before he met Lord Alfred — was his biblical tragedy of *Salomé,* which gave him an international reputation and which, indeed, as I am certain you all know, made his name a household word wherever the English language is not spoken.

True, he did not follow the ancient story, as one might say, step by step. Indeed, he elaborated its brief and terrible outline with the fanciful notion that Salomé, daughter of Herodias, Princess of Judea, demanded the head of the prophet Jokanaan, or John the Baptist, as a reward for her dancing because she was enamoured of the holy man and because the holy man rejected her. Now this invention — for, of course, it is nothing more than an invention — has proved so popular since the play was written that today, in such undisputed centres of Scriptural interpretation as Hollywood, Salomé's overwhelming passion for John the Baptist is accepted by millions of people as being, in every sense of the word, a gospel fact.

In this strange play that seems to have been wrought out of moonlight and jewels and blood, the daughter of Herodias dances before her amorous step-father Herod the Dance of the Seven Veils, and makes her demand — Herod, Tetrarch of Galilee, is filled with terror by what he hears and to the Princess, in place of the head of the prophet, he offers first a great emerald bestowed on him by Caesar, then his hundred milk-white peacocks, and finally all the jewels of his treasure house. And as Oscar Wilde, one of the few Irishmen, though not the only one, to have written a play in French, did in fact compose *Salomé* in that language, I would like to describe to you something of Herod's offering of jewels in its original form.

The Jewish Princess, having danced under the full moon, makes her request. 'Donnez-moi la tête de Jokanaan. . . .'

'Non, non, vous ne voulez pas cela. Vous me dites cela

seulement pour me faire de la peine, parce que je vous ai regardée pendant toute la soirée. Eh bien, oui. Je vous ai regardée pendant toute la soirée. Votre beauté m'a troublé. Votre beauté m'a terriblement troublé, et je vous ai trop regardée. Mais je ne le ferai plus. . . . Il ne faut regarder que dans les miroirs, car les miroirs ne nous montrent que des masques. . . . Oh! Oh! du vin! j'ai soif. . . . Salomé, Salomé, soyons amis. Ecoutez. J'ai des bijoux cachés ici que même votre mère n'a jamais vus, des bijoux tout à fait extraordinaires. J'ai un collier de perles à quatre rangs. On dirait des lunes enchainées de rayons d'argent. On dirait cinquante lunes captives dans un filet d'or. Une reine l'a porté sur l'ivoire de ses seins. Toi, quand tu le porteras, tu seras aussi belle qu'une reine. J'ai des améthystes de deux espèces. Une qui est noire comme le vin. L'autre qui est rouge comme du vin qu'on a coloré avec de l'eau. . . . J'ai des saphirs grands comme des œufs et bleus comme des fleurs bleues. La mer erre dedans, et la lune ne vient jamais troubler le bleus de ses flots. J'ai des chrysolites et des béryls, j'ai des chrysoprases et des rubis, j'ai des sardonyx et des hyacinthes et des calcédoines et je vous les donnerai tous, mais tous, et j'ajouterai des autres choses. . . . Salomé. . . . J'ai un cristal qu'il n'est pas permis aux femmes de voir et que même les jeunes hommes ne doivent regarder qu'après avoir été flagellés de verges. Enfin, que veux-tu, Salomé? Dis-moi ce que tu désires et je te le donnerai. Je te donnerai tout ce que je possède, sauf une vie. Je to donnerai le manteau du grand prêtre. Je te donnerai le voile du sanctuaire.'

'Donnez-moi la tête de Jokanaan. . . .'

'Qu'on lui donne ce qu'elle demande! C'est bien la fille de sa mère.'

It was on the twelfth of February in the year of grace, 1895, Oscar Wilde sent a telegram to one of his most devoted and loyal friends, Mrs. Ada Leverson, the fashionable writer, whom he always called 'The Sphinx'.

'Dear Sphinx: Can you come tonight to the theatre 7.45. dress rehearsal without scenery bring Robbie or someone with you have secured small box for you for first night Oscar.'

The first night in question was the first night of that new comedy of his about which he felt so securely certain that during rehearsals, on being asked by a newspaperman did he think it was going to be a success, he had answered: 'But it is, the most enormous success. What remains to be seen,' he added, 'is will the audience be . . . a success?'

The Importance of being Oscar by this time meant, of course, the Importance of not being Ernest, and we all, I think, remember bits and pieces of that indescribably complicated little plot. I have no intention of going into that, I promise you, faithfully, but I would like you to remember that, in it, a charming, cultivated, rather serious, rather earnest young gentleman, respected in the County of Hertfordshire as Mr. John Worthing, and, for subtle reasons of his own, known to his friends in London as Mr. Ernest Worthing, is in love with the Honourable Gwendolen Fairfax to whom he offers honourable marriage. He is caught red-handed, as you might say, in the very act of proposing, by Gwendolen's mother, Lady Bracknell, who, sailing unannounced into the drawing-room and seeing there the young gentleman kneeling at her daughter's feet, says to him briefly: 'Rise, sir, from this semi-recumbent posture. It is most indecorous.'

Gwendolen, with that elaborate girlish simplicity for which she is so justly famous and feared, especially by her girl friends, says: 'But I am engaged to Mr. Worthing, Mama.' Mama, like Queen Victoria, is not amused, and to her daughter she replies:

'Pardon me, you are not engaged to anyone. When you

do become engaged to someone, I, or your father, should his health permit him, will inform you of the fact. An engagement should come on a young girl as a surprise, pleasant or unpleasant as the case may be. It is hardly a matter that she could be allowed to arrange for herself. . . . And now I have a few questions to put to you, Mr. Worthing. While I am making these enquiries, you, Gwendolen, will wait for me below in the carriage. . . .

'In the carriage, Gwendolen, the carriage! . . . You may take a seat, Mr. Worthing.'

'Thank you, Lady Bracknell, I prefer standing.'

'I feel bound to tell you that you are not down on my list of eligible young men, although I have the same list as the dear Duchess of Bolton has. We work together in fact. I am quite ready to enter your name, should your answers be what a really affectionate mother requires. Do you smoke?'

'Well, yes, I must admit I smoke.'

'I am glad to hear it. A man should always have an occupation of some kind. There are far too many idle men in London as it is. How old are you?'

'Twenty-nine.'

'A very good age to be married at. I have always been of the opinion that a man who desires to get married should know either everything or nothing. Which do you know?'

'I know nothing, Lady Bracknell.'

'I am pleased to hear it. I do not approve of anything that tampers with natural ignorance. Ignorance is like a delicate exotic fruit: touch it and the bloom is gone. The whole theory of modern education is radically unsound. Fortunately, in England at any rate, education produces no effect whatsoever. If it did, it would prove a serious danger to the upper classes, and probably lead to acts of violence in Grosvenor Square. What is your income?'

'Between seven and eight thousand a year.'

'In land, or in investments?'

'In investments, chiefly.'

'That is satisfactory. What between the duties expected of one during one's lifetime, and the duties exacted from one after one's death, land has ceased to be either a profit or a pleasure. It gives one position and prevents one from keeping it up. That is all that can be said about land.'

'I have a country house with some land, of course, attached to it.'

'A country house! How many bedrooms? Well, that point can be cleared up afterwards. You have a town house, I hope? A girl with a simple, unspoiled nature like Gwendolen could hardly be expected to reside in the country.'

'Well, I own a house in Belgrave Square.'

'What number in Belgrave Square?'

'149.'

'Ah, the unfashionable side. I thought there was something. However, that could easily be altered.'

'Do you mean the fashion, or the side?'

'Both, if necessary, I presume. What are your politics?'

'Well, I am afraid I really have none. I am a Liberal Unionist.'

'Oh, they count as Tories. They dine with us. Or come in the evening at any rate. And now to minor matters. Are your parents living?'

'I have lost both my parents.'

'To lose one parent, Mr. Worthing, may be regarded as a misfortune. To lose both looks to me like carelessness. Who was your father? He was evidently a man of some wealth. Was he born in what the Radical papers call the purple of commerce, or did he rise from the ranks of the aristocracy?'

'I'm afraid I really don't know. The fact is, Lady Bracknell, I said I had lost my parents. It would be nearer the truth to say that my parents seem to have lost

[42]

me. . . . I don't actually know who I am by birth. I was
. . . well, I was found.'

'Found?'

'The late Thomas Cardew, an old gentleman of a very
charitable and kindly disposition, found me and gave me
the name of Worthing, because he happened to have a
first-class ticket for Worthing in his pocket at the time.
Worthing is a place in Sussex. It is a seaside resort.'

'Where did the charitable gentleman who had a first-
class ticket for this seaside resort find you?'

'In a handbag.'

'A handbag?'

'Yes, Lady Bracknell. I was in a handbag — a somewhat large, black leather handbag, with handles to it —
an ordinary handbag in fact.'

'In what locality did this Mr. James, or Thomas Cardew come across this ordinary handbag?'

'In the cloakroom at Victoria Station. The Brighton
line. . . .'

'The line is immaterial. Mr. Worthing, I confess I feel
somewhat bewildered by what you have just told me. To
be born, or at any rate bred, in a handbag, whether it
had handles or not, seems to me to display a contempt
for the ordinary decencies of family life that reminds one
of the worst excesses of the French Revolution. And I
presume you know what that unfortunate movement led
to? As for the particular locality in which the handbag
was found . . . well! you can hardly imagine for a moment
that I or Lord Bracknell would dream of allowing our
only daughter — a girl brought up with the utmost care
— to marry into a cloakroom, and form an alliance with
a parcel? Good morning, Mr. Worthing!'

The first night of *The Importance of Being Ernest* — the last first night as Mrs. Leverson, the Sphinx, has called it —was on St. Valentine's Day, the fourteenth of February, 1895, at St. James's Theatre, London, and it was, of course, a triumphant success. The author was now at the zenith of his career. Aesthete, poet, scholar, sage, philosopher, essayist, novelist, critic, dramatist, wit, a happy husband, the father by this time of two fine boys . . . life was full and rich, and exquisite and absurd. And the air in St. James's Theatre that night was golden, warm, rippling with laughter, radiant and scented, though outside the London night was very cold and very dark. And outside the theatre the Marquis of Queensberry who for a long time had been protesting vainly and violently against the friendship of his son Bosie — Lord Alfred Douglas — with the famous dramatist, turned furiously away to drive home alone through the ominous night. He had been prevented by the police from entering the auditorium, and had left at the stage-door, in Oscar Wilde's name, a bouquet composed, presumably by himself, not of flowers at all, but of cauliflowers, carrots, onions, turnips and other useful domestic vegetables, and this he had intended to hurl, with suitably insulting epithets, at the head of the man he hated most in the world. Lord Queensberry was always hating somebody, it was his hobby, but at the moment it happened to be Oscar Wilde. Having failed about the vegetarian bouquet, the Marquis — the screaming, scarlet Marquis as Wilde called him — left some days later an open card for his enemy at the Albemarle Club of which both he himself and Wilde were members, and on the card his Lordship had scribbled a few libellous and, incidentally, wrongly spelt words. And when, again a few days later, Wilde, calling casually at his Club, read what the Marquis had written on the open card that had been handed to him by a porter, he sent a brief letter to a friend who has not yet entered our story tonight; but he was the most devoted, loyal, faithful and completely courageous friend that any man could hope to find. He was a Scottish-Canadian by the name of Robert Ross. And this is the letter that Wilde wrote to him on that occasion.

'My Dearest Robbie,
 Since I saw you something has happened. Bosie's father has left an open card at my club with hideous words on it. I don't see anything now but a criminal prosecution. My whole life seems ruined by this man. The tower of ivory is assailed by the foul thing. On the sand is my life spilt. Robbie, I don't know what to do. If you can come here at 11.30 please do so tonight. I mar your life by trespassing on your love and kindness. I have asked Bosie to come tomorrow.

Yours ever,
OSCAR'

🐦

The actor, in silence, takes the green carnation from his coat, regards it for a moment and lets it fall to the ground as the light fades out.

THE CURTAIN FALLS

*The trials of Oscar Wilde
are presumed to have
taken place during the interval*

PART TWO

De Profundis

'. . . Oscar Wilde and Alfred Taylor, the crime of which
you have been convicted is so bad that one has to put
stern restraint upon oneself to prevent oneself from describing, in language which I would rather not use, the
sentiments which must rise to the breast of every man of
honour who has heard the details of these two terrible
trials — it is of no use for me to address you. People who
can do these things must be dead to all sense of shame,
and one cannot hope to produce any effect upon them.
It is the worst case I have ever tried. . . . That you, Wilde,
have been the centre of a circle of extensive corruption of
the most hideous kind among young men it is impossible
to doubt. . . . I shall, under such circumstances, be expected to pass the severest sentence that the law of
England allows. In my judgement it is wholly inadequate
for such a case as this. The sentence of the Court is that
each of you be imprisoned and kept to hard labour for
two years.'

There was a brief silence with some odd cries of
'Shame! Shame!' and suddenly Oscar Wilde cried out:
'And I? May I say nothing, my lord?'

Mr. Justice Mills in reply flapped an impatient hand
at the warders who hurried the two prisoners — the poet
and the pimp — out of sight. Out of sight and out of
mind, and outside the Old Bailey, on the paving stones of
Fleet Street, London, prosperous citizens and public pros-
titutes danced together in virtuous triumph. The 'Nineties
of the Green Carnation were dead and done for forever:
the mood of *The Yellow Book* was destined now to make
way for the reign of the Yellow Press.

And yet . . . one cannot help wondering if Wilde had
been allowed to speak at that moment what would have

happened? Would he have delivered from the dock some speech comparable in eloquence and in power to that of the Irish rebel leader Robert Emmet: a speech that, independently of his own fate, might have revealed the strange and uniquely Anglo-Saxon quality of the law that had sentenced him? It is impossible to say. Indeed, to my mind, the only tragic surviving remainder of the whole saga is that still today, and still to so many thousands of people today, the name of Oscar Wilde merely conjures up an immediate image of shame and scandal. It is time not to forget the scandal or the shame but to place them in their correct relationship with his subsequent development as an artist and a human soul.

The indescribable anguish he endured was bound, of course, to pluck some expression from him sooner or later, and it did, as we know, in a letter he wrote from Reading to his friend Lord Alfred Douglas.

When the letter was finished his bosom was cleansed, as he himself said, of 'much perilous matter': so much so indeed that some of the old unconquerable gaiety of heart began to flicker forth again: and this is remarkably in evidence in the instructions he gave to the faithful Robert Ross about the disposal of the longer letter he had addressed to Lord Alfred.

'My dear Robbie,' he writes to Ross from Reading on the first of April 1897:

'I send you a MS. separate from this, which I want you to have carefully copied for me — You see, Robbie, if you are going to be my literary executor, you must be in possession of the only document that gives any explanation of my extraordinary behaviour. . . . Some day the truth will have to be known — not necessarily in my lifetime — but I am not prepared to sit in the grotesque pillory they put me into for all time. . . . I do not defend my conduct, I explain it.'

'As regards the mode of copying, Robbie . . .' he continues: 'I think the only thing to do is to be thoroughly modern and to have it type-written. Of course the MS. should not pass out of your control, but could you not get Mrs. Marshall to send down one of her typewriting girls — women are the most reliable as they have no memory for the important — to do it under your supervision? I assure you that the typewriting machine, when played with expression, is not more annoying than the piano when played by a sister or any near relation. Indeed, many among those most devoted to domesticity prefer it. The lady typewriter might be fed through a lattice in the door, like the Cardinals when they elect a Pope, till she comes out on to the balcony and can say to the world: "Habet Mundus Epistolam"; for indeed it is an Encyclical letter, and as the Bulls of the Holy Father are named from their opening words, it may be spoken of as the *Epistola: in Carcere et Vinculis.*'

However, the letter written from Reading by Oscar Wilde to Lord Alfred Douglas in the spring of 1897 is now known to the world as *De Profundis*.

HER MAJESTY'S PRISON
READING

'Dear Bosie,

After long and fruitless waiting I have determined to write to you myself, as much for your sake as for mine, as I would not like to think that I had passed through two long years of imprisonment without ever having received a single line from you, or any news or message even, except such as gave me pain. . . .

'Our ill-fated and most lamentable friendship has ended in ruin and public infamy for me, yet the memory of our ancient affection is often with me, and the thought that loathing, bitterness and contempt should forever take the place in my heart once held by love is very sad to me.

'I have no doubt that in this letter which I have to

[49]

write of your life and of mine, there will be much that will wound your vanity to the quick. If it prove so, read the letter over and over again till it kills your vanity. Do not be afraid to read it. Remember that the supreme vice is shallowness. Everything that is realised is right. . . .

'I will begin by telling you that I blame myself terribly. As I sit here in this dark cell in convict clothes, a disgraced and ruined man, I blame myself, I blame myself for allowing an unintellectual friendship, a friendship whose primary aim was not the creation and contemplation of beautiful things, entirely to dominate my life. . . . From the very first there was too wide a gap between us. Of the appalling results of my friendship with you I do not speak at present. I am thinking merely of its quality while it lasted. It was intellectually degrading to me. Those incessant scenes that seemed to be almost physically necessary to you and in which your mind and body grew distorted and you became a thing as terrible to look at as to listen to: that dreadful mania you inherit from your father, the mania for writing revolting and loathsome letters; your entire lack of any control over your emotions; these things were the origin and cause of my fatal yielding to you in your daily increasing demands. You wore me out. . . . The letter I received from you on the morning of the day I let you take me down to the Police Station to apply for that ridiculous warrant for your father's arrest was one of the worst you ever wrote, and for the most shameful reason. . . . You and your father! . . . between you both I had lost my head. My judgement forsook me. Terror took its place. Blindly I staggered as an ox to the shambles. Those of my friends who really desired my welfare implored me to retire abroad, and not to face an impossible trial. You forced me to stay, to brazen it out in the box by absurd and silly perjuries. At the end, of course, I was arrested and your father became the hero of the hour. His place is among the kind, pure-minded parents of Sunday school literature; your place is with the infant Samuel; and in the lowest mire of Malebolge of Hell I sit between Gilles de Rais and the Marquis de Sade. . . . Of course, I discern in all our relations not Destiny merely, but Doom: Doom that always walks swiftly, because she goes to the shedding of blood. . . .

'I remember you sending me a very nice poem of the undergraduate school of verse for my approval: I reply by a letter of fantastic literary conceits: I compare you to Hylas, or Hyacinth, Jonquil or Narcissus, to some one whom the great God of Poetry favoured and honoured with his love. The letter is like a passage from one of Shakespeare's sonnets, transposed to a minor key.

'Look at the history of that letter! It passes from you into the hands of a loathsome companion: from him to a gang of blackmailers: copies of it are sent about London to my friends, and to the manager of the theatre where my work is being performed: every construction but the right one is put on it: society is thrilled with the absurd rumour that I have had to pay a huge sum of money for having written an infamous letter to you: this forms the basis of your father's worst attack. I produce the original letter myself in Court to show what it really is: it is denounced by your father's Counsel as a revolting and insidious attempt to corrupt your innocence (*the actor repeats, with quiet and bitter irony:*) to corrupt your innocence: ultimately it forms part of a criminal charge: the Crown takes it up: the Judge sums up on it with little learning and much morality: I go to prison for it at last. That is the result of writing you a charming letter.

'Some paper, the *Pall Mall Gazette*, I think, describing the dress rehearsal of one of my plays, spoke of you as "following me about like my shadow". The memory of our friendship is the shadow that walks with me here: that seems never to leave me: that wakes me up at night to tell me the same story over and over till its wearisome

[51]

iteration makes all sleep abandon me till dawn: at dawn
it begins again: it follows me into the prison yard and
makes me talk to myself as I tramp round and round:
each detail that accompanied each dreadful moment I
am forced to recall: there is nothing that happened in
those ill-starred years that I cannot recreate in that cham-
ber of the brain that is set apart for grief or for despair:
every strained note of your voice, every twitch and gesture
of your nervous hands, every bitter word, every poisonous
phrase comes back to me and I remember the street or
river down which we passed: the wall or woodland that
surrounded us, at what figure on the dial stood the hands
of the clock, which way went the wings of the wind, the
shape and colour of the moon. . . . You and I have known
each other for more than four years. Half of the time we
have been together: the other half I have had to spend
in prison as the result of my friendship with you. . . .

'How clearly I saw it all then, as now, I need not tell
you. But I said to myself: "At all costs, I must keep love
in my heart. If I go into prison without love what will
become of my soul?" The letters I wrote to you at that
time from Holloway Gaol were my effort to keep love as
the dominant note of my own nature. I could if I had
chosen have torn you to pieces with bitter reproaches. I
could have rent you with maledictions. I could have held
up a mirror to you, and shown you such an image of
yourself that you would not have recognised it as your
own till you found it mimicking back your gestures of
horror, and then you would have known whose shape it
was and hated it, and hated yourself for ever. . . . More
than that indeed, as you well know. The sins of [here,
to make clear an historical fact which in this form, as
Wilde wrote it, has appeared obscure to many playgoers,
I have added that the actor may pause and say:] The
sins of . . . no, I will simply say "of another". *You will
know well who that other was*. . . . The sins then, of . . .

[52]

another were being placed to my account. Had I so chosen I could on either trial have saved myself at the expense of that other, not from shame indeed, but certainly from imprisonment. Had I cared to show that the Crown witnesses—the three most important witnesses—had been carefully coached by your father and his solicitors, not in reticences merely, but in assertions, in the absolute transference, deliberate, plotted and rehearsed, of the actions and doings of that other onto me, I could have walked out of the Court with my tongue in my cheek and my hands in my pockets, a free man. I did not choose to do that. . . . I have never regretted my decision for a single moment, even in the most bitter periods of my imprisonment. But Bosie, do you really think that you were worthy of the love I was showing you then? Or that for a single moment I thought you were? . . .

'Sorrow after sorrow has come beating at these prison doors in search of me: they have opened the gates wide and let them all in.Hardly, if at all, have my friends been allowed to see me. My enemies have had full access to me always: twice in my public appearances in the Bankruptcy Court; and twice again in my public transferences from one prison to another have I been shown, under conditions of unspeakable humiliation, to the gaze and mockery of men. . . . The messenger of Death had brought me his tidings of my mother and gone his way; and hardly has that wound been dulled — not healed — by time, when violent and bitter and harsh letters come to me from my wife's solicitors. I am at once taunted and threatened with poverty. That I can bear. I can school myself . . . after what I have suffered . . . to endure worse things than poverty; but now my two children are taken from me by legal procedure. That the law should decide, and take it upon itself to decide, that I am one unfit even to be with my own children is something quite horrible to me. . . . I envy the other men who tread the prison

yard along with me. I am sure that their children wait
for them, look for their coming, will be sweet to them. . . .

'The poor are wiser, more charitable, more kind and
infinitely more sensitive than we are. . . . In their eyes
prison is a tragedy in a man's life, something that calls
for sympathy in others. They speak of a man who is in
prison as of one who is "in trouble" simply. It is the phrase
they always use, and the expression has the perfect wisdom of love in it . . . of love and sorrow.

'And where sorrow is, believe me, there is holy ground.
. . . There indeed is the spirit and the image of Jesus
Christ Himself. I know that now . . . but I know too that
everything about my tragedy has been hideous, mean,
repellent, lacking in style; our very dress makes us grotesque. We are the zanies of sorrow. We are clowns whose
hearts are broken. We are specially designed to appeal to
the sense of humour. Listen . . . on the thirteenth of
November, 1895, I was brought here to Reading from
London. From two o'clock till half past two on that day
I had to stand on the central platform of Clapham
Junction in convict dress, and handcuffed, for the world
to look at. I had been taken out of the hospital ward
without a moment's notice being given to me. Of all
possible objects I was the most grotesque. And when
people saw me they laughed. Each train as it came up
swelled the audience. Nothing could exceed their amuse-
ment. And that was, of course, before they knew who I
was. As soon as they had been informed . . . who I was
. . . I was spat upon . . . and then they laughed still more.
For half an hour I stood there in the grey November rain
surrounded by a jeering mob.

'And for a year after that was done to me I wept:
every day at the same hour and for the same space of
time. . . . Now, remember, that is not such a tragic thing
as possibly it sounds to you. To us who lie in prison tears
are a part of every day's experience. A day in prison on

which a man does not weep is a day on which his heart is hard, not a day on which his heart is happy. . . .

'I remember that as I was sitting in the dock on the occasion of my last trial listening to Frank Lockwood's appalling denunciation of me — appalling: like something out of Tacitus, like something out of Dante, like Savonarola's denunciation of the Popes of Rome — and being sickened with horror at what I heard, suddenly the thought came to me: how splendid it would be if I was saying all this about myself. I saw then at once that what is said about a man is nothing. The point is, who says it. Who? . . . Man's very highest moment is, I have no doubt at all, when he kneels in the dust, and beats his breast, and tells all the sins of his life. And so with you. So with you . . . you would be much happier if you let your mother know a little at any rate of your life: from yourself. And do not be afraid. Do not allow sentimentality to hinder you. . . . Remember that the sentimentalist is invariably a cynic at heart. Indeed, sentimentality is merely the bank-holiday of cynicism. And delightful as cynicism is from its intellectual side . . . in itself it can never be more than the perfect philosophy for the man without a soul, for to the true cynic, nothing is ever revealed. . . .

'Of course I know that to one so modern as I am, *enfant de mon siècle*, merely to look at the world will be always lovely. I tremble with pleasure when I think that on the very day of my leaving prison both the laburnum and the lilac will be blooming in the gardens, and that I shall see the wind stir into restless beauty the swaying gold of the one, and make the other toss the pale purple of its plumes so that all the air shall be Arabia for me. . . .

'Ah! But all trials are trials for one's life, just as all sentences are sentences of death; and three times have I been tried . . . so that Society, as we have constituted it, will have no place for me, can have indeed no place to offer. . . . I seem to have passed from one moment of fame into an eternity of infamy . . . and I know that until I die I shall be an outcast; as outcast as the leper.

'But Nature, whose sweet rains fall on unjust and just alike, will have clefts in the rocks where I may hide, and secret valleys in whose silence I may weep undisturbed. She will hang the night with stars for me so that I may walk abroad in the darkness without stumbling, and send the wind over my footprints so that none may track me to my hurt: she will cleanse me in great waters, and with bitter herbs make me whole.

'And incomplete, and imperfect as I am, yet from me you may have still much to gain. You came to me once long ago — do you remember? — to learn the pleasure of art and the pleasure of life. Well, perhaps now I am chosen to teach you something much more wonderful: the meaning of sorrow and its beauty.

Your affectionate friend,

OSCAR WILDE'

Yet there were moments, even in the blackest hours of his prison life, in which the incurably blithe spirit of his humour came dancing forth. One of his warders had a taste for reading, a very kindly man whose name was Tom Martin. He hailed, as I have learned quite lately, from Belfast, our Northern capital, where they speak the English tongue with a very strange accent — stranger perhaps than our own accent when we speak that same tongue in the south — so I hope you will be able to follow without too much difficulty the gist of a conversation between Warder Tom Martin and his distinguished prisoner when the warder said:

'Excuse me, Mr. Wilde, sir, but — er Charles Dickens, sir — now mind you, Mr. Wilde, I'll admit to you frankly

I don't really care much for Dickens myself, the print is too small, but it seems that the critics of his own day regarded him as a kind of a wee god or something — now the critics of today, I mean of our own time, do you think that by them would he be considered a really great writer, now, sir?'

'Charles Dickens? Oh yes, of course. . . . You see he is dead.'

'Oh, I see, sir. Yes, sir. I hadn't thought of that. Dead, eh? Like Shakespeare. Yes, I see what you mean. Well now what about Mr. John Strange Winter, sir — the greatest English novelist living today as he was described in my Sunday paper last week — what would you say yourself about him, sir?'

'What would I say about Mr. John Strange Winter? . . . Well, to begin with, dear friend, you must know that Mr. John Strange Winter happens to be a lady. Yes, and I believe a most beautiful and charming lady. And I would much rather talk to her than read him.'

'Och, well, you live and learn. So Mr. John Strange Winter is a female is he? Oh God forgive him! . . . seems unnatural to me. . . . Well now, er, excuse me detaining you I'm sure sir, but on the subject of lady writers, what about Miss Marie Corelli? I mean, would Miss Marie Corelli be considered like a really great lady writer, sir?'

There was a delicate pause. Then Wilde said gravely: 'Now don't think for a moment that I have a word to say against the moral character or reputation of Miss Marie Corelli. But from the way she writes, she ought to be here instead of me.'

🍂

Oscar Wilde was released from prison on the twenty-third of May 1897, and among those who gathered to welcome him at the house of the Reverend, and indeed heroic,

Stuart Headlam, was his old friend the Sphinx, Mrs. Ada Leverson. There she was, loyal to the last, as elegant and lovely as ever, and the only lady present. So of course it is she who has left us what is the most vivid description of this re-union: 'We all felt acutely embarrassed,' she confesses, 'at the mere idea of seeing poor Oscar again. But when Oscar came in he at once put us at our ease. He came in with the dignity of a king returning from exile. He came in talking, laughing, smoking a cigarette, with newly-waved hair and a flower in his button-hole and he looked markedly better, slighter and younger than he had looked two years previously. His first words were: 'Sphinx, my dear Sphinx! . . . It is a cold, gold May morning', he went on. 'Sphinxes are minions of the moon and yet you get up at dawn to greet me. And my dear Sphinx,' he went on, 'how brilliant of you to know exactly the right hat to wear at seven o'clock in the morning to meet a friend who has been away! You can't have got up, you must have sat up!'

He talked on lightly for some time, then wrote a letter, and sent it in a hansom cab to a Roman Catholic Retreat, asking if he might retire there for six months. While waiting, he lounged in a corner of the sofa quite in his old grand, bland manner, smoking cigarette after cigarette, and presently he said to Mrs. Leverson: 'Sphinx, do you know one of the dreadful punishments that happens to people who have been "away"? They are not allowed to read *The Daily Chronicle*! Did you know that? Coming along I begged to be allowed to read it in the train. Impossible! Then I suggested I might perhaps be allowed to read it upside-down. To this, to my enormous astonishment, they consented. . . . And so, dear Sphinx, all the way from Reading to London I read *The Daily Chronicle* upside down and I never enjoyed it so much in all my life. It is really the only way to read newspapers.'

Presently the man returned with the letter but it contained disappointing news. The Retreat replied in no uncertain terms that they could not possibly accept Mr. Wilde into their establishment on what they described as his 'impulse of a moment'. He must think seriously about the matter, they assured him, for at least a year. . . . In fact they shut their door against him.

When he had read the letter he broke down suddenly and completely and wept, Mrs. Leverson tells us — these are the Sphinx's own words now — 'poor Oscar wept with all the bitter abandon of a child. I learned later,' she continues, 'that he left for his beloved France later that afternoon, accompanied by the devoted Robert Ross and by another faithful friend, Reginald Turner.' He never set foot in England — or, indeed, in his own Ireland — again.

But in the late summer of that same year 1897, the great French writer, André Gide, who had known Wilde intimately for years, called on him and found him living on the outskirts of a remote fishing village called Berneval on the Norman coast, and here, Gide tells us, he found the Irish poet in a subdued but mysteriously happy frame of mind, enchanted by the place — its loneliness and even its desolation seemed to fill him with joy — and also with an extraordinary determination to live there for the rest of his life.

'Now I know André, that I can never leave Berneval again,' he said, 'I never want to. Prison has completely changed my imagination,' he continued. 'I was relying on it for that. . . . The mere thought of great cities like Paris and London fills me with terror. Oh, I could never go back to the old life. . . . Why? . . . You ought to know, my dear André. I told you my secret years ago: that I had put my genius into my life, my talent only into my writing. My life is my masterpiece. My life is a work of art, and, my dear fellow, no artist should ever resume his labours on the same work in the same manner, or it would

[59]

seem as though the fundamental design was not a complete success. . . . Besides, I have learned now what pity is. Pity . . . I never understood it before, but now it seems to me a thing of such unutterable beauty that I thank God — oh, yes, André, quite literally — I thank Him every night and every morning for having taught me something of the meaning of pity. Even if I had to go to prison to learn it. . . . It was well worth while, well worth while. André,' he said suddenly, 'would you like to give me a great pleasure? Send me a life of Francis of Assisi. Yes, send me the best life of St. Francis you can find. . . . Why he more than another saint? Oh well, I feel, you see, that it was Francis who found the road I may be meant to follow, if I can. If I have the strength. Who knows?' he ended the conversation suddenly, 'I might do worse things with the end of my work of art, don't you agree?'

Now Oscar Wilde, as we can guess, never even posed as being a consistent man. Consistency was not among the virtues he admired: indeed there is a legend that he once included it in his list of what he called the seven deadly virtues. Yet I feel convinced that the lonely, mystical St. Francis period at Berneval—one might call it the Franciscan epoch — was perfectly and consistently sincere, as long as it lasted. The only trouble was that it did not last very long; any more than his tender admiration for the village of Berneval where he was going to live until the day of his death, lasted very long. 'I shall go raving mad if I stay in this ghastly little hole one day or night longer! It is killing me' (always a favourite phrase, even when he was a boy in Dublin). 'It is killing me with boredom.'

Even his righteous indignation against Lord Alfred Douglas did not last long, and you have heard something of the consistent violence and bitterness of that from the few pages you have heard from *De Profundis*. But it did not last, for he went back to him. Oh, fatally, of course, and against all the warnings of his friends. But he did go back in the autumn of that same year—1897—rejoining him in Italy, at Posilipo in Naples, where Lord Alfred had a villa by the sea. It was in that house, the Villa Giudice, that Wilde completed the poem that was to be his last work.

He had gone back to poetry, you see, and to a poetry of a startlingly new form for him. No more elaborate serpentine rhythms or hidden rhymes, no more glowing images of ivory and gold and precious stones: all now was deliberately plain and so simple that a child could understand it. And all imbued with the spirit of pity he had learned, as he said to André Gide, in prison.

He did not dedicate this poem to any intimate friend, as was his custom, but to an English soldier with whom he had never exchanged a single word. The soldier had been sentenced to death for the murder of his own unfaithful wife and he was hanged in Reading on the morning of seventh July 1896. To his memory Wilde dedicated the poem that he called *The Ballad of Reading Gaol.*

He did not wear his scarlet coat,
For blood and wine are red,
And blood and wine were on his hands
When they found him with the dead,
The poor dead woman whom he loved,
And murdered in her bed.

He walked amongst the Trial Men
In a suit of shabby grey;
A cricket cap was on his head,
And his step seemed light and gay;
But I never saw a man who looked
So wistfully at the day.

I never saw a man who looked
With such a wistful eye
Upon that little tent of blue
Which prisoners call the sky
And at every drifting cloud that went
With sails of silver by.

I walked, with other souls in pain
Within another ring,
And was wondering if the man had done
A great or little thing,
When a voice behind me whispered low,
'That fellow's got to swing.'

Dear Christ! the very prison walls,
Suddenly seemed to reel,
And the sky above my head became
Like a casque of scorching steel;
And, though I was a soul in pain,
My pain I could not feel.

I only knew what hunted thought
Quickened his step, and why
He looked upon the garish day
With such a wistful eye;
The man had killed the thing he loved,
And so he had to die.

Yet each man kills the thing he loves,
By each let this be heard,
Some do it with a bitter look
Some with a flattering word.
The coward does it with a kiss,
The brave man with a sword!

*

Some love too little, some too long,
Some sell, and others buy;
Some do the deed with many tears,
And some without a sigh:
For each man kills the thing he loves,
Yet each man does not die.

He does not die a death of shame
On a day of dark disgrace,
Nor have a noose about his neck,
Nor a cloth upon his face,
Nor drop feet foremost through the floor,
Into an empty space.

He does not wake at dawn to see
Dread figures throng his room,
The shivering Chaplain robed in white,
The Sheriff stern with gloom,
And the Governor all in shiny black,
With the yellow face of Doom.

*

So with curious eyes and sick surmise
We watched him day by day,
And wondered if each one of us
Would end the self-same way,
For none can tell to what red Hell
His sightless soul may stray.

*

We sewed the sacks, we broke the stones,
We turned the dusty drill:
We banged the tins, and bawled the hymns,
And sweated on the mill:
But in the heart of every man
Terror was lying still.

[63]

So still it lay that every day
Crawled like a weed-clogged wave:
And we forgot the bitter lot
That waits for fool and knave
Till once, as we tramped in from work,
We passed an open grave.

*

Then back we went, with soul intent
On Death and Dread and Doom:
The hangman, with his little bag,
Went shuffling through the gloom.
And I trembled as I groped my way
Into my numbered tomb.

That night the empty corridors
Were full of forms of Fear,
And up and down the iron town
Stole feet we could not hear,
And through the bars that hide the stars
White faces seemed to peer.

*

At last I saw the shadowed bars,
Like a lattice wrought in lead,
Move right across the whitewashed wall
That faced my three-plank bed,
And I knew that somewhere in the world
God's dreadful dawn was red.

With sudden shock the prison-clock
Smote on the shivering air,
And from all the gaol rose up a wail
Of impotent despair,
Like the sound that frightened marchers hear
From some leper in his lair.

And as one sees most fearful things
In the crystal of a dream,
We saw the greasy hempen rope
Hooked to the blackened beam,
And heard the prayer the hangman's snare
Strangled into a scream.

And all the woe that moved him so
That he gave that bitter cry,
And the wild regrets, and the bloody sweats
None knew so well as I:
For he who lives more lives than one
More deaths than one must die.

*

The warders strutted up and down,
And watched their herd of brutes,
Their uniforms were spick and span,
And they wore their Sunday suits,
But we knew the work they had been at,
By the quicklime on their boots.

For where a grave had opened wide,
There was no grave at all:
Only a stretch of mud and sand
By the hideous prison-wall,
And a little heap of burning lime,
That the man should have his pall.

For he has a pall, this wretched man,
Such as few men can claim:
Deep down below a prison-yard,
Naked for greater shame,
He lies, with fetters on each foot,
Wrapt in a sheet of flame!

*

And all the while the burning lime
Eats flesh and bone away,
It eats the brittle bone by night,
And the soft flesh by day.
It eats the flesh and bone by turn,
But it eats the heart alway.

For three long years they will not sow
Or root or seedling there:
For three long years the unblessed spot
Will sterile be and bare,
And look upon the wondering sky
With unreproachful stare.

They think a murderer's heart would taint
Each simple seed they sow.
It is not true! God's kindly earth
Is kindlier than men know,
And the red rose would but blow more red,
The white rose whiter blow.

Out of his mouth a red, red rose!
Out of his heart a white!
For who can say by what strange way
Christ brings His will to light,
Since the barren staff the pilgrim bore
Bloomed in the great Pope's sight?

*

They hanged him as a beast is hanged:
They did not even toll
A requiem that might have brought
Rest to his startled soul,
But hurriedly they took him out,
And hid him in a hole.

[66]

The Chaplain would not kneel to pray
By his dishonoured grave:
Nor mark it with that blessed Cross
That Christ for sinners gave,
Because the man was one of those
That Christ came down to save.

Ah! happy they whose heart can break
And peace or pardon win!
How else may man make straight his plan
And cleanse his soul from Sin?
How else but through a broken heart
May Lord Christ enter in?

                    *

In Reading Gaol by Reading Town
There is a pit of shame,
And in it lies a wretched man
Eaten by teeth of flame,
In a burning winding-sheet he lies
And his grave has got no name.

And there, till Christ call forth the dead
In silence let him lie:
No need to waste the foolish tear,
Or heave the windy sigh:
The man had killed the thing he loved,
And so he had to die.

And all men kill the thing they love,
By all let this be heard,
Some do it with a bitter look,
Some with a flattering word,
The coward does it with a kiss,
The brave man with a sword!

The re-union of Oscar Wilde and Alfred Douglas did not endure. Many circumstances both sordid and tragic forced them to part again, and for a long time Wilde drifted about in Europe, mainly in Italy, mainly alone: a derelict in the prime of life. His wife Constance died at Genoa: stricken, when he heard the news of her sudden illness, by grief and despair, he hastened to her side but he was too late even to say good-bye.

He covered her grave with red roses and drifted south again, alone again, to Rome, to Naples, and to Sicily. But Paris was to be his ultimate and I think inevitable destination: Paris with her beauty, her time-worn airs and graces, her often grim and always experienced smile, and her greatest gift, her least widely known and most precious secret gift of infinite compassion.

He wrote no more. Like Socrates, he talked — oh, not as wisely but as well — and although death was so much closer than he realised, he did live for a few more months in Paris, in the Latin Quarter in a small hotel whose proprietors, Monsieur and Madame Dupoirier, evinced for him the most tender, touching, poetical and practical kindness and friendship. He was quite comfortable and might perhaps have found some happiness there but for one small thing that barred all happiness from him as long as he remained within those four walls, and that was the wallpaper. The wallpaper was tough. A design of remorseless and repellent aspect, it seems, was carried out with unwavering firmness in three colours, shades or tints. Magenta and Magenta and Magenta. And every time poor Wilde looked at it — which had to be pretty often as he was there so much — he would give vent to his favourite slogan: 'It's killing me, Robbie, killing me!' Once, with a half sad, half comic resignation, as though he sensed his days were numbered, he gazed fixedly at the offending wallpaper and murmured: 'Yes, of course. One of us had to go.'

One night — it was his last outing — sitting at a café on the Boulevard des Italiens with those few remaining friends who cared or dared to be seen with him, he said suddenly: 'I am going to tell you a little fable. It is called *The Doer of Good* and so, of course, it is horribly sad.

'Night fell on a purple city and He was alone. And in a street of that city He saw one whose face and raiment were painted and whose feet were shod with pearls. And behind her came, slowly as a hunter, a young man whose eyes were bright with lust.

And He laid His hand on the young man's shoulder and He said to him: 'Why do you look at this woman and in this wise?'

And the young man turned and recognised Him, and he made answer and said: 'I was blind, and you gave me sight. At what else should I look?'

And He moved swiftly forward and touched the painted raiment of the woman and He said to her: 'Is there no other way to walk save in the way of sin?'

And the woman turned and recognised Him, and she laughed with joy and said: 'But you forgave me my sins. And the way is a pleasant way.'

And He went forth from the purple city.

And when He had passed through the gates of the city He saw seated by the roadside a man who was weeping.

And He laid His hand on the man's head and He said to him: 'Why are you weeping?'

And the man looked up and recognised Him and he made answer and said: 'Lord! I was dead, and you raised me from the dead. What can I do now but weep? My Lord, My Lord!'

◆

The poet's last days in Paris, like that fable of Christ and Lazarus, were strange and sad enough. Physically he suffered very greatly, sometimes thrusting his hand into his mouth to prevent himself from crying out with the pain. It is a source of sincere comfort to many people to remember that towards the end the faithful Robert Ross called in a priest, a Passionist father, who baptised and received the Protestant-born Irishman, Oscar Fingal O'Flahertie Wills Wilde into the Catholic Church and finally gave him Extreme Unction. He died peacefully, and slowly, very slowly, after his death his name, which for so many years had remained silent in the world, or was spoken only in shameful or bawdy whispers, began, through the gradual re-appearance of his books — his fairy tales, his incomparable essays on art and life, his poems, his stories and his plays — his name began once more to sound like a bell in the world of Art and Letters.

And to the end he retained, not a little but a great deal, of the old incorrigible wilfulness and gaiety of his temperament. Indeed, it is said that on the morning of the day before he died he looked up at Robert Ross with a sudden gleam in his eyes and whispered: 'Robbie . . . when the Last Trumpet sounds, and you and I are couched in our purple and porphyry tombs, I shall turn and whisper to you: "The Last Trumpet! But Robbie," I shall add: "Robbie, dear boy, pray let us pretend we do not hear it. . . ." '

THE END

D/C 20/12/78